lost in the milky way

a collection of poems

Emmie Vale

Paperback ISBN: 978-1-0699023-2-0

E-book ISBN: 978-1-0699023-3-7

Contents

To the perfection seekers who had to slay that part of themselves when they became a parent.

***

You are not alone. Not then, not now, not ever.
Let this be your proof that it *will* get better.

To My Daughter

Baby girl, if you are reading this, I need you to know without a doubt that you were never the cause of my unhappiness. Your arrival on Earth did precipitate the rapid decline of my mental health at the time, but the core of my issues, the tears in the tapestry of my soul, existed long before the idea of you was ever tangible.

You see, some learn early on how to share their feelings, how to cope with hardship, how to ask for help. I did not. No one prevented this psychological growth from happening, I simply took it upon myself to make the weight of my presence as small as possible, to be self-sufficient in every sense of the term.

After two and a half decades of emotional self-isolation, enforcing the mirage that I could do it all on my own, I crumpled. Not because of you, not because of your dad, not because of anything or anyone.

For the first time in my life, I was faced with a challenge, the most important one of my life, one I could not undertake on my own. Yet, instead of listening to everyone who was offering to help, to share the load with me, I pushed them all away.

Incapacity to excel at motherhood on my own was a failure, one set by my own over-achieving, toxic standards.

All this to say, this is my story, my words, fuelled by powerful destructive thoughts that almost lead to my permanent demise.

Baby girl, you were never the cause for my despair. You were the catalyst for change, propelling me to face the long list of issues I was blinded to. I can't say that you saved me, it wouldn't be fair to the baby version of yourself. That part is credited to your dad, my doctor, my therapists, my friends, and to myself. But I can say that you've forever inspired me to do better, to accept failure as a milestone towards change and growth.

Finally, if there's one thing I hope you'll learn from this raw collection of poems is that, regardless of it all, my love for you never wavered. It was the only constant. You were my lighthouse in the tumultuous hurricane of postpartum depression.

I've forever and will always love you.

- Mom

Before

---

it all went dark

before we begin

i want to tell this story
i need to tell it right
the tale of motherhood
from before til the end

my end
my impending death
a terrible wish to escape
the endless pile of guilt
the months, the years, of sleepless nights
the demise of my individuality

then comes
the sliver of hope
to find light through it all
to live for more
to survive your child
to survive your mind
finding your way back to more
to love, to breathe, to exist

for them
because of them
but most of all
for myself

day one

she was here right on time
on her own terms
actually, three days late

she marred my skin
and marked my soul

an era ended
while another began
at the exact moment
she took her first breath

love at first sight

i'm in awe

her wrinkled face
one perfect pout

the red birthmark
on her left ankle

her fluffy red hair
a genetic heirloom

her strong fingers
forever fisting my collar

her tiny hungry wails
equally powerful and soft

mama bear

i would lie
i would die
i would kill

anything
for my daughter
anything
to protect her

the first sight of love

the sum of two imperfect humans
created the most wonderful creature

it's truly tragic
that you'll never
see yourself
through my eyes
never witness how
undeniably
perfect you are

rebirth

part of me died
the day she was born
my heart outgrew itself
exploding, rearranging
making room for
an endless well
infinitely filled to the brim
with incandescent love
for her, and her only

grateful love

i'll never be the parent
who'll berate her mercilessly
requesting grand-children
by the time she turns twenty
but i silently hope
she'll get to experience
the soul shattering,
heart-splitting,
life altering moment
when one holds
their newborn
for the very first time

an omen

her arrival should have foreshadowed
what was to ensue

the timing was not as i expected
the birth veered off course
the hospital stay was extended
the healing was slower than others

nothing was as i anticipated
instead of surfing the waves
i kept swimming against stormy currents

my stubborn mind was
already trying to redirect
to hold on to absent reins
when i should have understood
on the very first day
that i was meant to let go

<u>missing records</u>

in the pile of things
i wish i had done differently
there's only one regret

wishing there were
more evidence
of her birth
the first days
bursting with
pure joy

she, selfless

the true definition of selflessness
should picture a lone mother
the moment after giving birth

built her shrines
paint her on ceilings
erect monuments for her

she gives up sleep
then her hobbies
then her friends
finally herself

she forgets to eat
to take warm showers
to go on quiet walks
then everything else

but she never
forgets her children
gives up on them

praise mothers worldwide
for they've forgotten
how to be at the epicentre
of anyone's universe
especially their own

here, now

living in the moment
standing here
living now

i struggle to stop
the incessant flow of thoughts
that pours through my mind
that keeps me from being
here, now

i can't commence to slow down
the pace of my worries
the race to my goals
i can't project myself, and be
here, now

i want to root myself, like her
to marvel at the sight of all, like her
i want to pause and exist, like her
here, now

Stranded

---

through time and space

disappearance

a few painful
restless weeks
and then

suddenly
the freight train
hits me at once

the first of
numerous collisions
that eventually

would destroy
every single
shred of joy

i used to muster
those very first
few weeks

prelude

estranged struggles
those you ignore way too long
those you notice but won't accept
those attached to destructive pleasures
those so painful you have no other choice
but to be comfortable with them

a soul drowning
drenched in pain
soaked in sorrows
dipped in despair

this is how you feel
uncalibrated, unregulated
so much so
you've accustomed yourself
to laying on a bed of nails

as though the pain
is the only evidence
that you are even here
existing, alive

with that comes the possibility
the slight chance really
to someday feel whole again
to calibrate oneself
to reset it all
to stop the ache
to start being
and breathing free

tormented

becoming a parent
my most intense path

forced to either
team up with
your demons
or battle them,
head on

forced to decide what
you'll be for them
and how you will
forge them to be

giving yourself freely
without forsaking your core
while remaining whole

impatient

i will not
wait for joy
to stop feeling
sadness

it doesn't
have to be
one or the other
it can't be

where's the in between?

there has to be
shades i don't know
shades i have never seen
shades worth salvaging my soul for

unsensing

let me see
i've gone blind
to reality

let me listen
i can only hear
chaotic noises

let me savour
everything tastes
like dust and ashes

let me feel
my heart beats still
but barely, erratically

let me scream
my throat is clogged
with guilt, hurt, rage

free me
let me peak though
this darkened veil
suffocating my senses

balance

like dancing on a rope
above nothingness and chaos
i can't stand long
i can't keep calm

often i fall down
sometimes deep
too deep
where standing up
becomes impossible

these days
i have trouble
balancing it all,
out of breath
exhausted,
overwhelmed by
the pressure to perform,
saddened by
my incapacity to deliver

of balance
i know nothing
it no longer exists

battle one

i feel conflicted
pulled apart
between heart
and reason

i need to focus
on myself,
on my health,
on my soul

how?

<u>the core</u>

i am a helper, a caregiver
a shoulder-to-cry-on-provider
i gain energy from helping,
from teaching, and guiding

and then?

i get overly involved,
and i have difficulties
remaining detached

i care too much
overwhelmed with the need
to soothe their pain

i feed on everyone's problems
as a way to avoid mine

in the end
i'm a hypocrite
not a saviour

conundrum

how
can i save myself
and still help others?

how
can i care just enough
without giving it all away?

how
can i make them happy
while nurturing myself?

how
can i remain theirs
without running away?

opposites

selfless not self-free
one has given up so much, sacrificed
while the other made a choice to nurture

a plea

stop praising moms
that give it all up
as if that should be
the standard for all to follow

we are not made equal
we are not made the same
our strengths are all needed
to build our beautiful world

quit comparing her and her
pinning them against one another
as if motherhood was a race to win
instead of a journey to survive

blues

staring at those deep blue pools
which have begun to ice over

the colour of a troubled ocean
i would gladly drown in

my heart melts
but my soul wavers

tears stream down my face
hopelessness fills me up

the sea of my insecurities
keeling me overboard

imposter

i wander the streets
pinning a smile on
giving it away to all
avoiding their pity

my despair is too grand
for anyone to truly care
of what will become
of my fake smile

the dragon

fumes and fire
breathing and heaving
temperamental and impulsive
caged, but unchained

exasperation followed by impatience
repetition that goes unanswered
the momentum builds
my willpower shatters
and *it* takes over

losing my bearings
holding on to the edges of sanity and kindness
while it rages, throwing flames all around
melting my self-confidence
destroying all traces of gentleness
that existed moments prior

the dragon scares them
but it frightens me

as the last embers remain,
descending into its cave
preparing myself to fight it

what remains is the reflection
of who I've become
when i let *it* free

on the edge

i walk the line
between wanting to hurt
and wanting to improve

my steps falter
i wobble, losing my footing
almost falling into the abyss
staring at where i could be

not sure that i want to escape it
feeling like i deserve the fall
because she deserved better
than a mother like me

k.o.

i'm ok
i'm good
i'm fine
i'm great
i'm ok

yet

i've not been ok
i'm at my worst
i'm far from fine
i never feel great
i'm so not ok

relatable

some nights
i give myself
the time of one song
to wallow in self-pity

reminding myself
through my pain
i am not alone
i feel as miserable
but less lonely
sitting here
on the cold tile floor
my skin marred and wet
my arms crossed
self-hugged

some nights
i listen to one song
and i know
it could get better
maybe

a million pieces

how can i mend
a shattered soul
when i was never taught
to weld my own wounds?

my abc

angered
bothered
checked out
defeated
exhausted
frustrated
gone
haunted
irritated
jarred
knocked down
limited
minimised
neglected
over it
pestered
quarreled
riled up
saddened
terrified
unknown
vaulted
worried
x-out
yearning
zero

unbeknownst

what's need?
what's want?

too numb to know
too beaten up to care

blind future

the worst is knowing
it might never get better
regardless of the efforts
and time you dedicated

where is hope, then?

infinite

there is no mechanic
to fix that broken switch
no electrician
to establish connectivity
no doctor
to prescribe a remedy
no parent
to help me learn and grow
no one
to kiss away the guilt
no self-esteem
left to salvage

the expanse at which
my suffering grows
is infinite
for this state of despair
i have fallen under
is limitless

my dagger

desperately
needing to hurt
but never willing to
become anyone's villain

turning the sword
on myself
piercing the only heart
i can bear to harm

the one problem

will it be easier
in one or ten years?
will I stop feeling
like my whole world is ending?

when will that be exactly?
how long can i hold on
before my life crumbles down?

i cannot stay still
i cannot stand here
i cannot admit that
this was the best of me

i cannot stop it
i cannot control it
my mind keeps racing
the beast within is raging

but it's not your fault
you did nothing wrong
the only problem
is that i'm your mom

the pain of letting go

dropping this ball
before it decided
to drop me
creating the perfect
illusion of control
i have been craving

sans

what would you call
that feeling between
anger and disappointment,
avoidance and disinterest?

emptiness?
a void?

the dying leaves
scattered on the floor
of this bottomless pit
called my existence
rotting away the last
shreds of hope i had
while i float away
amongst nothingness

do i?

do i matter?
is there any difference
to my existing?
would anyone miss me
if i ever disappeared?

constantly pleasing
everyone around
effortlessly present
to help them all
forever holding their worlds
on my narrow shoulders

too much
it's too much
it's all too heavy

i'm exhausted
please lift it off of me
take it away
take it back

or i'll crumble

sacrifice

i've sacrificed
for so long
i don't know
the way back
anymore

measurements

where are the cups
the gallons, the rulers,
and the scales
to measure whether
i've given enough
done enough
said enough
sacrificed enough
to be enough?

metaphysical

when pain is spoken
the body listens
emulates, stricken

it erupts
hurt spills all over
my weakened state
now defeated

survivor

i am not self-reliant
out of choice
i had to be
it's the only way
i have known
to survive
so far

not many
have attempted
to prove
that i no longer
needed to be

the ten commandments of motherhood

you must be brave
and oh so strong

you must protect
heal, and always help

you must love yourself
and teach her to do as such

you must always be kind
especially to those who deserve it less

you must never lash out
or show the darkness simmering beneath

you must not cry too much
or be weak, uncontrolled

you must cope with the negativity
but without impacting anyone else

you must be reliable
even when all you want is to break

you must be available
even if you crave some peace and quiet

you must be the bigger person
and always rise above

- how? why?

my mirror

i was angry at her
for reflecting
my own flaws
for not regulating
her tiny feelings
when mine
were undoubtedly
raging,
untamed

six feet

i've been dying
instead of living

holding the shovel
instead of my family

on the edge of falling
instead of healing

i cannot die
but living hurts

shades

all encompassing
darkness and shadows
guilt-fuelled panic attacks

my soul,
a compass
leading south
fast

Escaping

---

responsibilities, reason, and reality

<u>on the verge</u>

i feel like a coward
for seeking an escape
for surrendering to sadness
for checking out on us

i am one foot out the door
the other suspended mid-air
awaiting further instruction
from my scattered brain

and you don't know
you don't seem to notice

open your eyes!
see me, feel this!
wrench me back inside,
shut the door, hold me tight!

if

if i was to leave
escape, or run away
to a far away land
you'd despise me
judge me selfish

if i was to end my life
quietly stop my beating heart
and end my inner turmoil
you'd be sad
you'd hate me

if i stay
keep pushing, trying my best
even when it's barely nothing
you'd be satiated
you'd carry on

how can i please you,
and tame my demons?
how can i be the one you need,
and not fall prey to *this* need?

what then?

what if it's not
about blame
but about strength
or my lack thereof
to entertain this charade
i've allowed to exist
to avoid confrontation
so as to not burden them

what if i'm done?
game over, i quit,
au revoir

suffering

absent
frozen in time
thoughts of death
invade my mind
bringing peace
a glimpse of
freedom

mad

the longer
you remove
anger
from your dialogue
it, with time,
will fester
burden your mind
a phantom cancer
the inoperable kind

muted

when was the last time
you let yourself scream?

safe

very few
made me
emotionally secure
enough to let
my feelings
roam free

to have and to hold

on days when
my heart is sore
my face drenched

i bring my left hand
to my right shoulder
and my right one
to my left side

then tighten my hold
giving myself the hug
i so desperately needed

missing

so forgettable
i've wondered if
they'd notice
my disappearance
if i ever go missing

or will i remain
the same ghost in death
i used to feel when alive

the impossible

don't be lazy
don't falter
do it all
do better
be better
be pretty
stand taller
stand out
stay kind
stay patient
never falter
never give up

*- f*ck that*

indecision

do i give up, or
do i try again?
was it a failure, or
did it not succeed yet?

am i a coward
for wanting to run away?
or would i be smart
for letting this go?

crossroads

people talk
about crossroads
to symbolize
the decision-making
choose road *a*
choose road *b*
move on

but what if
a and *b*
aren't on my map

what if
there's no choice
but to walk through dirt
climb sharp hills
and defeat the trolls
that haunt me

what if
the only choice
moving forward
is to suffer
the only way
to heal me
is to add
one final scar

coping

i have come to understand
that i don't have the right tools
to help manage my guilt

my first reflex,
whenever anger arises,
is to bottle it up, apologize,
to let guilt consume me
for being a terrible parent

i don't know how
to redirect my angst
to emulate the behavior
to become a role model
the right way

i need a default outlet
for my pent-up frustration
to bleed out my soul
to start fresh tomorrow,
instead of feeling like a dam
that's about to burst
any minute

the cost

i gave second chances
without setting clear boundaries
opening the door wide
for them to harm my peace
again, and again
and again

i will not

i can't ask them
to care for me better
when i've already asked
and never received validation

so, i won't

i can't demand respect
or help, or support
when they require
so much of it
themselves

so, i won't

i can no longer hope
for the love i crave
for the care i deserve
when they only scattered crumbs

so, i won't

the purpose

what is the point of living
if not to brand the world
with your flavour
in some kind of way?

why exist
if it's not to stand out
to someone, at something?

what's my purpose,
my goal?

what will my daughter
remember me by
if i were to leave tomorrow?

Landing

---

on her moon

hope

the emotion that gives strength
the one that leads people
to overcome the most difficult times
the one that gets me
to move forward in the morning
the only feeling that can reignite
the lost flame within

once you lose it
you lose your way
your purpose
the road ahead
becomes blurry
before it disappears

then,
one only has two choices
to give into despair,
let it all go,
wait for the pain
to, one day, decimate you

or,
to have faith in life
and in yourself
that, someday,
the fog will clear
if only you have the courage
to keep on walking

foolish

how i feel a fool
how wrong i was
waking up from a trance
the fog finally disappearing
the guilt and despair
the undeserving of their love
me pushing them away
to alleviate their burden

how i have been a fool
to dream of loneliness
to thirst of escaping it all
to tap out
and leave
far, far away

in therapy

sadness is granted
tears are common
anger is allowed
face your fears out loud
disappointment can happen
discussions of guilt-trips encouraged

it will tire you
it will enlighten you
it will bring you hope
it will help you grieve
it will lighten the load

but be patient, be kind
your mind is cluttered
with an invisible sickness
that has many cures
none of which will solve
anything overnight

make some noise

you have a voice
you have a choice

say it
take it
make it
choose it
do it

don't give away
a freedom
that was so hard
for women to earn

the other mothers

if comparison is the thief of joy
then indifference is the thief of
resentment, anger, and jealousy

which one will you let through
the iron gates of your mind?
choose one, choose wisely

all i ask of you

love me
at my best, but also at my worst

choose me
to be your number one sidekick

fight for me
on the days i'm too weak to fight for myself

need me
use loud words and louder actions

stay with me
even when we're angered or discouraged

hug me
often, especially when you feel me pull away

cry with me
hold me, wipe my tears, kiss them away gently

be silent with me
words are not mandatory, but your presence is

help me save myself
by holding my hand, by being patient

feel

please love, cherish
please cry, weep
or be desperate
but please, i implore
feel something
feel everything
deep and hard

for living
without feeling
is dull
so don't settle
for a life
in shades of grey
when you could rejoice
in all colours and shades

speak up

be strong enough
to admit that
you need help

be brave enough
to accept it
when offered

be humble enough
to understand
that you cannot
do it all alone

be your one

to the one
who lost
her sense
of self

you're not lost
you're lonely

forgetting
whose opinion
to value most
to measure
your worth

living

your best
doesn't need
to be great

being average
shouldn't be
a failure

being just ok
can be enough
for today

you don't have
to thrive
to be worthy

but you do
have to try
for life to be
worth it

duet

there is no good
without hurt
nor happiness
without tragedy

open up
to all that is bright
when you have it

but try
to hold on to the ship
as it becomes wreckage

remember that
all feelings are fleeting
they all shall pass
nothing is permanent

disappointment

in my book
happiness is simple
it's to grasp the opportunities
to spend time with your people
it's to create moments
and to go on adventures with them

it's also to nurture yourself
mind, body and soul
it's to appreciate the little things
to remember that moments are temporary
the good as well as the bad ones

so, soak it all in
rejoice in what you have
but keep on making a conscious effort
to plan your joy

no one said it'd be easy
but it's the only way i can live
without disappointing myself
once more

be

be ordinary
don't over-apologise
be strong enough to recognise your mistakes
and proud enough to not easily bow down to others

be ordinary
smile even if all your teeth aren't straight
look for the little glimpses of joy
and when your day is truly shitty
look up to the sunset or find the moon and the stars
they'll always shine on you

be ordinary
wear your pyjamas all day
or that cute matching set you bought
or dress up and wear all the make-up
but wear what gives you the confidence
to power through your day

be ordinary
enjoy your day, live a little messy
skip the dishes and laundry
tonight's chores will always wait for you
but deep clean if you must
sometimes a cleaner house
helps declutter one's mind

be ordinary
say hello and goodbye to coworkers
smile to strangers for no reason
go get your favourite treat
kiss your kids goodnight
call your relatives once in a while

but
learn not to over do it
learn to say “no”
learn to set boundaries
learn to be kind to yourself

no one else
can show you
as much mercy
as *you* could

round two

you lost that battle
the one raging inside
the darkness threw the first punch
and it came out the victor

now

will you choose to stand up?
will you curl up on yourself,
and let it win?

or

will you stand up straighter,
up your defence,
and brace yourself for round two?

drop the balls

there are just so many things
one can hold on to
before they break

so many balls can fit
in the crook of your arms
before you inevitably
drop them all

choose
calculate
organise
prioritise

as for the rest
let them go,
drop them all

only hold on to
what you must

f*ck

we're allotted
a set number
of daily fucks to give

once you've chosen
to spend them all
your body has to supply
extra mental energy

that's when
you feel tired,
then strained,
then low,
then depressed,
then burned out.

the solution?
stop swearing in traffic,
the cars won't move faster.
don't curse mother nature,
none can control the weather.

don't always focus on tomorrow's problems,
try to be safe and prepared,
spend more time living in today
than anguished about what's to come

free

the moment I chose
to let go
of all that couldn't
be perfect
my anger
evaporated

joy

a symptom
of a healthy soul
nurtured by itself
and the ones it chose
to entrust its heart to

not a goal
to be achieved
but a current
flowing freely
as waves
of contentment
come and go

progress

when i chose to roll my eyes
i now lower my gaze to hers

when i chose to grunt, annoyed
i now take a few breaths, eyes closed

when losing made me go mad
i now take frequent pauses, unbothered

lesson learned

everyone's problems
don't have to be
your problems

- you can't save them all, save yourself first

meditation

i used to despise meditating
my mind kept racing
wandering through every nook
scavenging for insecurities
hollering at all my fears

resulting in an endless stream,
an onslaught of negative thoughts
which made me forget to breathe
and judge myself for ten minutes

i still don't quite enjoy meditating
but i've stopped hating myself
through this tedious process
of breathing and observing

i count and acknowledge
my fears, my struggles
instead of letting them
take over my world
unconscious and above

rightful

becoming proud
the hardest path
one has to walk

learning to differentiate
being proud
to being vain
being bubbly
to being exuberant
being conscientious
to being intense
being clumsy
to being annoying
being disciplined
to being ruthless

becoming proud
is accepting
which one you are
at your core

pride

be proud of
the little victories,
tiniest accomplishments

those grains of sand
will add up to a whole beach

worthy

self-confidence
is the knowledge
that your worth
isn't found in
whether or not
you can succeed
but in knowing
you're as great
either way

improving

never cease to
desire and aim for
a better version of yourself

the alternative
is terrifying for
everyone who loves you

mantra

you are important, you matter
you are important, you matter
you are important, you matter
you are important, you matter
you are important, you matter

keep repeating it, until it sticks

player one, fight

you're a worrier
but be a warrior

push through
all that fear
all the hurt

fight back
and conquer

louder, please

i've said it to myself
felt it in my marrow
and now i scream it
from all the rooftops

choosing
yourself
is
not
selfish

be the person you wish they'd become
pave that path, however it looks like
change that narrative for yourself
so they can grow looking up to you
instead of counting down the days before
they can move the hell away from you

from me to me

i write this to you
but to me first

you are entitled to your emotions
practice sharing them freely
without restraint or filters
without deceit or lies

look at yourself
stare at the beautiful
reflection of a worthy soul
and speak your truth
loud and clear
let it out alone first

take the time
to purge your heart
of the pain it feels
to discover privately
the root of the issue

and then stand
and find strength
to get back up
to make it better

I count to one

---

bonus

one

i have one child
she's one
my one
my only child
but she's not
just one

she's enough
even more so
she's all
and then some

so don't
pity her
spite me
curse us
judge us
as you don't
know the reason

i'm done
justifying
a decision
that has nothing
to do with anyone
the aftermath
ours to bear
alone

to grieve nothing

it's been years
since the moment
we decided
to not have more

that final day
silent tears
streamed,
relentlessly

why

only one
why only?
she's one
not lonely

she's ours
she's all
chosen
cherished

explained

there are
reasons why
i won't bear
another child

reasons why
i won't go
through it again

reasons why
my body can't
do round two

regardless
not wanting to
should be reason enough

it's not for them
to decide
not for them
to judge

it's not because
my way
isn't their way
that it's not
the right path
for us

<u>ours</u>

why is it selfish
to choose one
when it's also
a choice
to have two
or more
or none?

best before

being a parent
has no expiration date
it's not for 18 years

it's for forever
it's for life
yours and theirs

while some
have never stopped
to consider the impact
of bringing another
into this messed up world

i have stressed
we have discussed
i cried
we argued
i pondered
we decided
unanimously

the guilt

sibling-less
she will be
we know
what we're willingly
withholding from her

i have had
two built-in best friends
in shapes of brothers
i have been mourning
what she won't experience
i have been compensating
for all its absence

thus
you need not guilt-trip us
we're way ahead of you

<u>the pros</u>
we've never had difficulties finding a babysitter
for one, many are available

since she turned one
we have mostly been able
to sleep throughout the night

her hand-me-downs are still in great condition
i love that i can give back to friends and family

at a young age
she has learned to have stretches of independent play
now, her imagination fascinates me

he and i can actually have nights to ourselves
to recharge our mental battery
to enjoy our hobbies, on a weekly basis

she's not an add-on
she's the conclusion

on the contrary

i am not judge and jury
especially towards others' choices

i will not state my way is better
because it might not be for you

motherhood can't be one size fits all
where you have to pick a lane blindly
while consciously accepting that
you'll never gain absolution in your choice

misplaced

i kept justifying our choice, often using the phrase "just one" when asked how many children i chose to bear

i've realised my angst was fuelled by fear to be judged by a society that prepackages and promotes so many possibilities for families of four while mine counts as three

i've realised i felt ashamed from not being able to please my family, his family, with an additional bundle of joy, from choosing to protect my peace instead of continuing to be their catalyst for pride

i've realised that, as long as i allow this sentiment to be anchored in whatever they may all feel, i will never be able to grieve that choice, i will never be able to fully be at peace

and so, i did

the next best

i believed day one was the happiest
of my whole entire life
but on day 25, you smiled
then on day 97, you said *maman*
and on day 416, you walked
this year on day 2,412, you read a storybook

being an influencer
to your growth may be
my greatest responsibility
but bearing witness
to each of your milestones
is my greatest honour

for that,
i will never forsake your existence
i will never curse the darkness
that plagued my mind for years

i feel pride that, like you,
i'm overcoming challenges,
the greatest conqueror of all

until the next hurdle
until the next best day

in the end

my greatest accomplishment is not that you were born, that i became a mother, or that i overcame post-partum depression

that was pure biology, a combination of him and me, mixed with the societal norms breathing down my neck, followed by a global pandemic

this was not 100% on me

it is not the pride and joy that i get to wake up next to my best friend, the man i trust with every single part of my soul

that was pure dumb luck, followed by many conversations, arguments and a succession of choices to remain each other's partner

this, also, was not 100% on me

my greatest accomplishment is learning to enjoy defeat and failure, to accept the bruises instead of fighting against loss or chaos

it's learning to embrace imperfections, new roads, redefining a future i had willingly frozen in time, allowing myself to step into multiple roles, and then changing the goals when they don't fit today's narrative

my greatest accomplishment is that i have yet to accomplish anything at all, not really, i am embracing this journey, and, while its final destination is too sombre to dwell on, i try not to

so,
i choose to live
i choose to write
i choose to try again
i choose to let go
i choose to forgive
i choose to love

and that
is 100% on me

Acknowledgements

Where do I begin to give thanks?

My life, like yours, has been a tapestry of events and decisions, friends and foes, love and resentment, chaos and pure bliss.

Becoming a parent was my biggest dream since I was of age to conceive, years before it was reasonable to start thinking about it, and over a decade before I actually became pregnant with my first, and only baby.

This is usually the section where you thank everyone who has influenced this book in any way shape or form.

For this book, I do not know how to do it. To be quite honest, I don't even want to thank myself for it.

The harshest poems exist mostly because I suffered, they are the living proof of scars I can't show, scars no one saw.

Let's do this one differently, shall we? Because I don't feel morose, I don't hide beneath masks, and I don't feel stormy clouds cluttering my mind anymore.

Instead, I wish to use this space for us all to take a long lasting look through our own distorted lens, and see all that you are.

Acknowledge your imperfections, treat them with care, cherish them instead of trying to hone something that can't.

Acknowledge your needs, the basic ones as well as the dreams. Make room in your schedule to spend time with yourself, with like-minded people, honing your crafts, solo-dating the one in the mirror.

Acknowledge when you are overwhelmed, voice it to whomever you can. You will find more open arms than you'd think. You would want to be there for them, wouldn't you? So why would it not be true when the situation is reversed?

Acknowledge that your fear of rejection has kept you from seeking help, that you can choose to do things while being afraid. Step over it, cradle it in your arms if you must, but don't stop on its account. Fear isn't meant to paralyse you, it's meant to teach you to protect yourself, OR to question its validity altogether.

Acknowledge that you matter. And if you don't find people who can teach you self-love, therapy is an appropriately hyped way to go about this one, you don't even have to be brave to let your soul bleed out in front of a qualified stranger.

To everyone reading this, thank you. My words mean nothing without your eyes, without your kind words of encouragement, without our shared experiences.

Hugging you all from afar,

Emmie

About the Author

Emmie Vale is a French-Canadian author who writes wholesome contemporary romance as well as emotional poetry. She likes when a book makes her go through a wide array of emotions, and she hopes her words made you feel those too.

She comes from a very small town in southern Quebec near Maine, but now lives near the national capital region of Ottawa with her witty husband and strong-willed daughter.

When she's not writing, you'll find her playing with her daughter, listening to audiobooks while going on long walks, daydreaming about quitting her day job to write full time, planning her next trip, having anxiety induced cleaning sprees, or spending her paycheck at local bookstores.

Instagram: **@emmievale.writes**

Also by Emmie Vale

Safe Spaces Series (Romance)

Holiday Haven (Book 1) - OUT NOW
Lessons Learned (Book 2) - September 2026
Dare Devil (Book 3) - January 2027

www.ingramcontent.com/pod-product-compliance
Lightning Source LLC
La Vergne TN
LVHW012110160826
845678LV00014B/3010

* 9 7 8 1 0 6 9 9 0 2 3 2 0 *